Contents

Looking at the night sky	4
Stars and constellations	6
The Solar System	8
The Moon	10
Mercury, Venus and Mars	12
Jupiter and Saturn	14
Uranus, Neptune and Pluto	16
Comets	18
Meteors	20
Eclipses and Auroras	22
Sky-watching	24
The northern skies	26
The southern skies	28
Night sky facts	30
Glossary	31
Index	32

Looking at the night sky

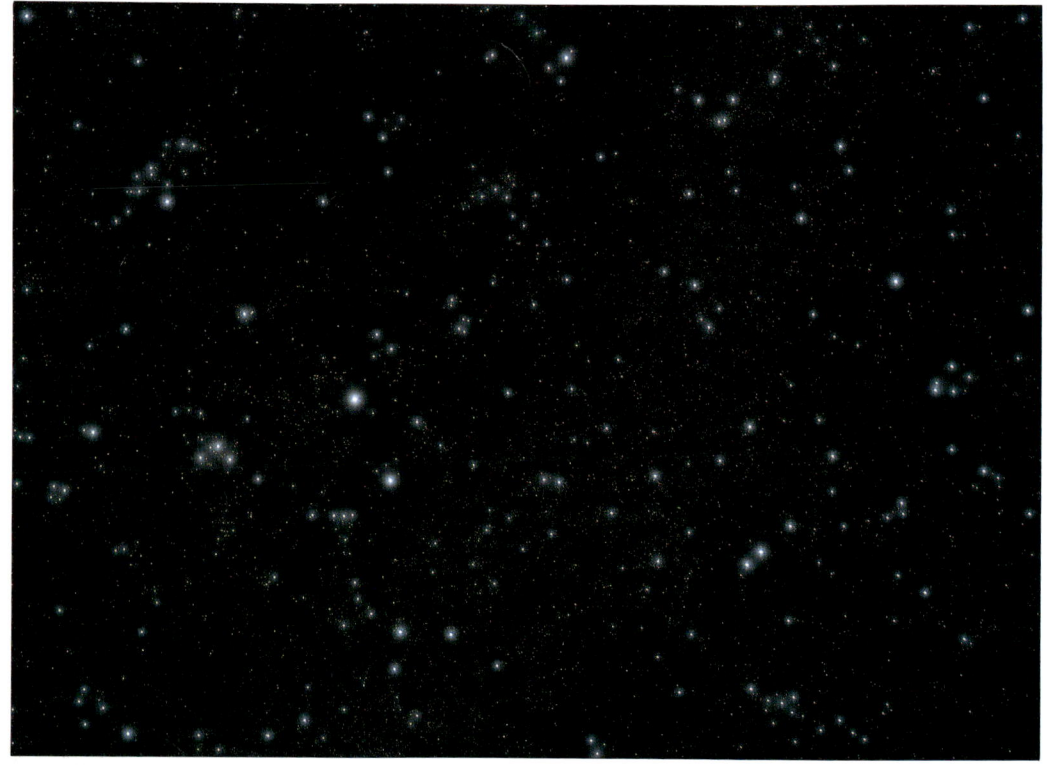

If you look up at the night sky on a clear night you will see a mass of shining stars. There are billions of stars in space, but most can only be seen with a telescope.

Each very large group of stars is called a galaxy. When you realize that there are millions of galaxies, you can begin to imagine the immense size of the Universe.

A distant galaxy.

Stars and constellations

Our galaxy, the Milky Way, is a spiral of over 100 billion stars, one of which is our Sun. Each star is a giant ball of flaming gas.

Our sun compared to the white star Rigel and the red star Aldebaran.

A constellation called the Pleiades.

Thousands of years ago people noticed that groups of stars formed patterns in the night sky. These patterns are called constellations. Many of them are named after ancient gods, heroes and animals.

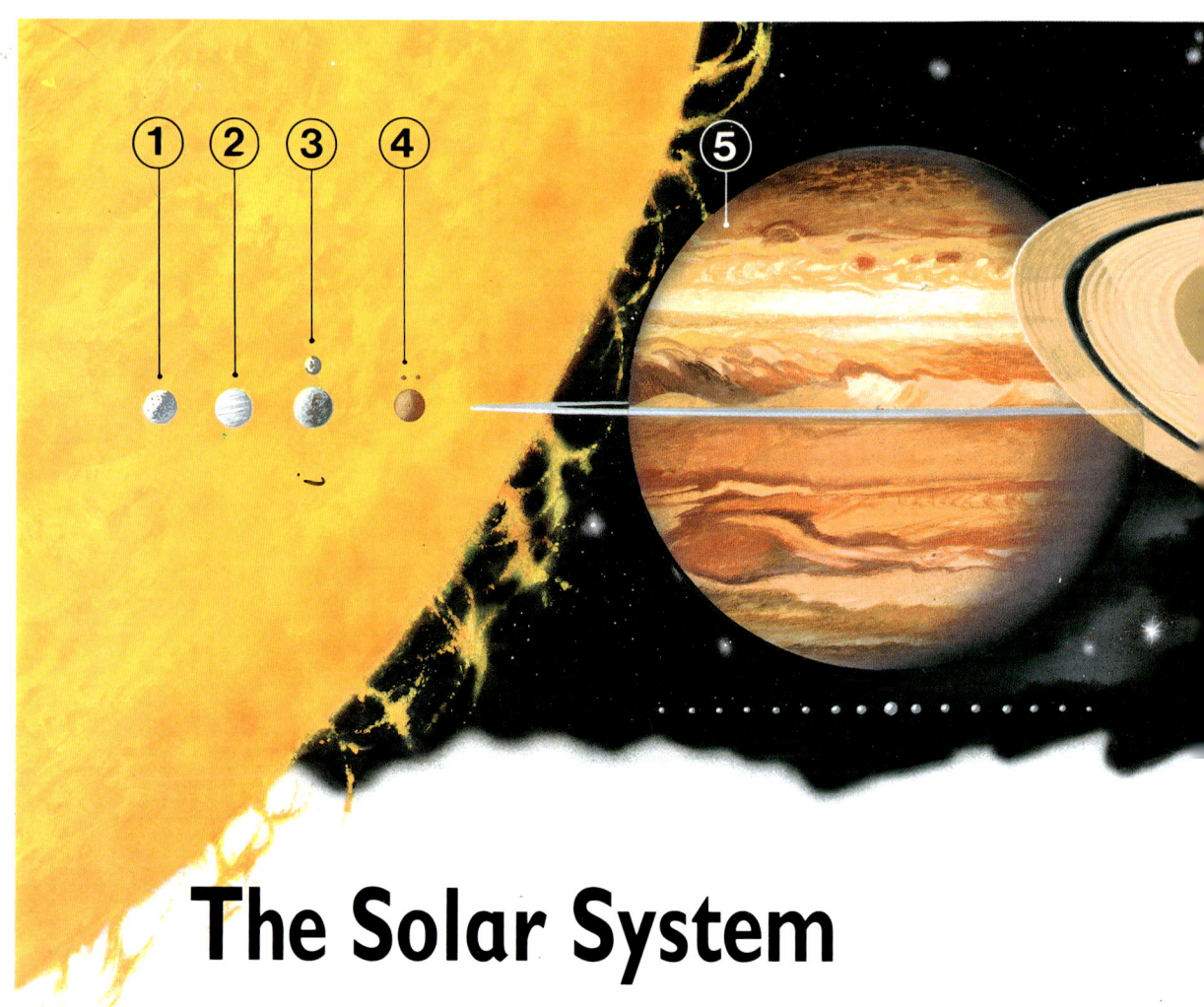

The Solar System

The Earth is one of nine planets that move around the Sun. Seven of the planets have moons which move around them. The Sun and its "family" of planets is called the Solar System.

These are the planets of the Solar System, shown to scale. The small dots show each planet's moons.

1 Mercury	4 Mars	7 Uranus
2 Venus	5 Jupiter	8 Neptune
3 Earth	6 Saturn	9 Pluto

The Moon

The Moon is only 384,000 km (239,000 miles) away from Earth. The Moon orbits (travels round) the Earth, making one orbit each month. The Moon has no light of its own, but as it travels, different parts of its surface are lit by light from the Sun. These changing views of the Moon are called its phases.

This map shows some of the features of the Moon.

Craters
1. Plato
2. Aristarchus
3. Kepler
4. Copernicus
5. Ptolemaeus
6. Alphonsus
7. Arzachel
8. Schickard
9. Clavius

Maria ("seas")
10. Sea of Rains
11. Sea of Serenity
12. Sea of Tranquillity
13. Sea of Crises
14. Sea of Fertility
15. Southern Sea

Mountains
16. Apennines
17. Haemus
18. Leibnitz

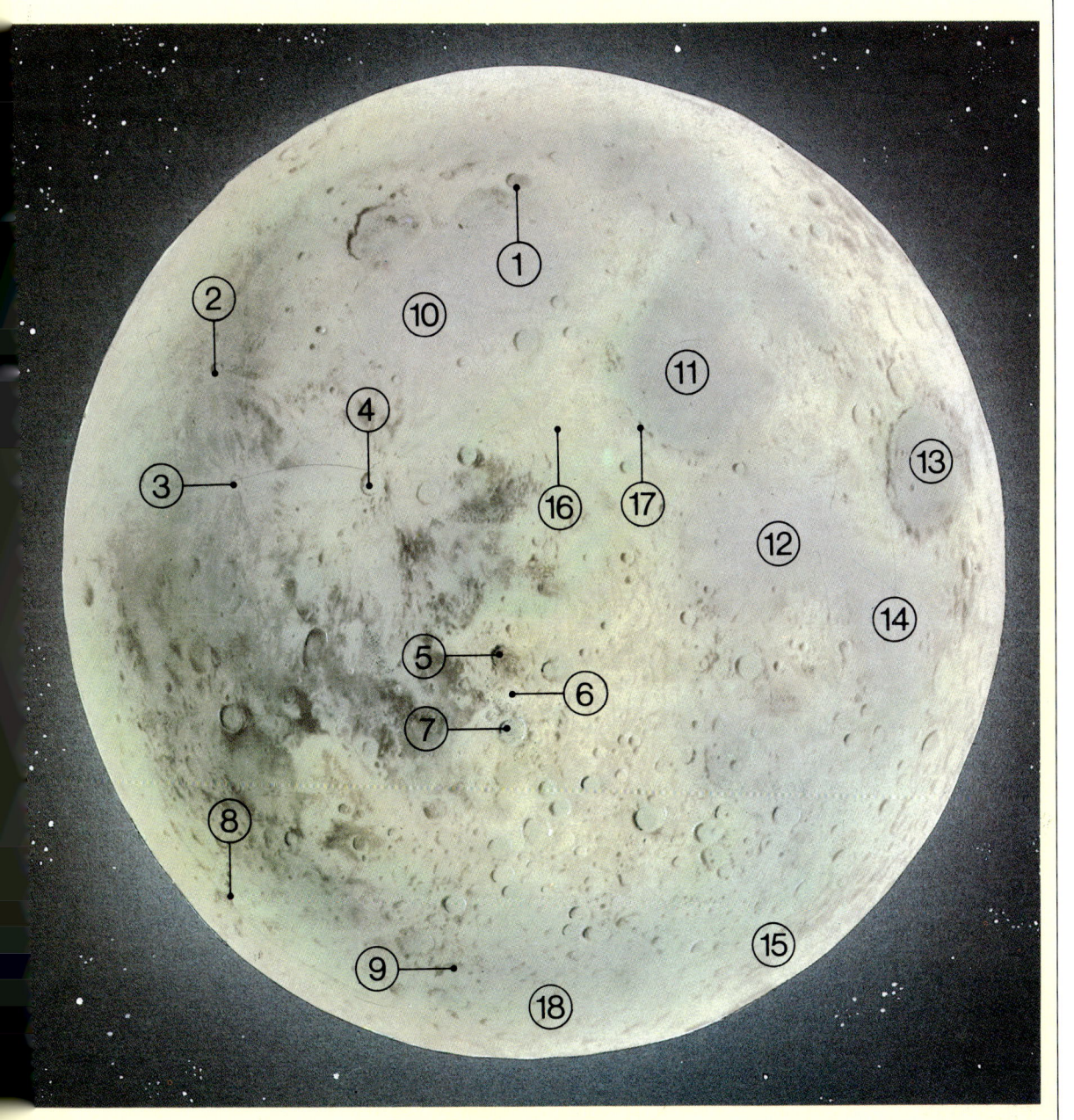

Mercury, Venus and Mars

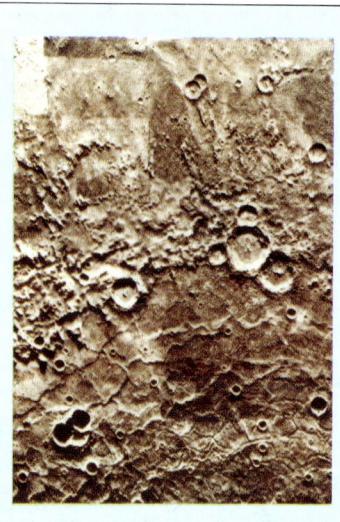

A photograph of the planet Mercury taken by a spaceprobe. The planet's surface is very hot and covered with craters.

Mercury, Venus and Mars are the planets nearest to Earth. Look for Mercury low in the western sky just after sunset, or low in the east just before sunrise. Venus is very bright, but no details on its surface can be seen because it is covered with thick cloud. Mars looks like a reddish ball when seen through a telescope.

Two unmanned spacecraft which landed on Mars in 1976 found it was a lifeless, rocky desert.

Venus is the same size as Earth. It is very hot and has a poisonous atmosphere.

Jupiter and Saturn

A photograph of Jupiter's Great Red Spot. The Spot is big enough to swallow two Earth-sized planets.

Jupiter is the largest planet in the Solar System. Its thick, dense atmosphere of hydrogen gas contains the Great Red Spot, a gigantic hurricane. Beyond Jupiter is Saturn, the ringed planet. It is much larger than Earth and, like Jupiter, has a hydrogen atmosphere.

**The spaceprobe *Voyager* cruises past Saturn.
The rings around the planet
are made of billions
of tiny lumps of ice.**

Uranus, Neptune and Pluto

Seen from Pluto, the Sun would seem no bigger than a very bright star.

These three planets, the furthest from the Sun, are all very cold. Uranus has some thin rings around it. It looks green because the atmosphere is made up of a green gas called methane. Neptune looks like a tiny blue disc when seen through a telescope. It has two moons. Pluto is about the size of our Moon. It is probably just a frozen ball of gas.

The *Voyager* 2 spaceprobe passed Uranus in 1986.

Voyager 2 is due to reach Neptune in 1989. Here you can see one of Neptune's moons.

Comets

Comets are rather like large dirty snowballs made from rocks, dust and ice. They wander through deep space, then heat up as they near the Sun. Their surface layers boil away into space forming a glowing tail millions of miles long.

Halley's Comet is the most famous. It has been known for over 1,000 years and comes close to the Sun every 75 years. It returned in 1986. Spaceprobes flew through the comet's tail measuring and photographing it.

The spaceprobe *Giotto* nearing the tail of Halley's Comet.

Meteors

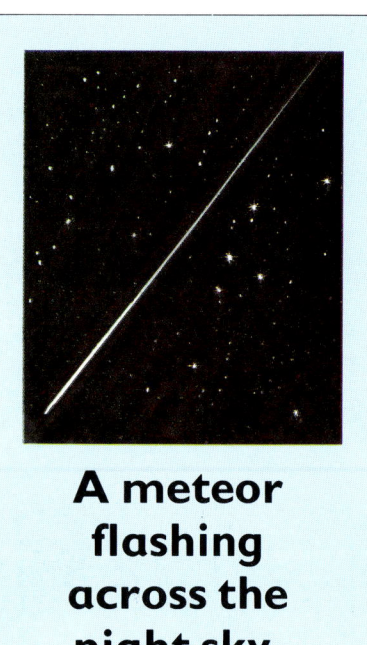

A meteor flashing across the night sky.

If you see a sudden streak of light falling across the night sky, it is probably a meteor. Most meteors are very small, about the size of a grain of sand. They are pieces of rock that have broken away from comets. They usually burn up as they enter the Earth's atmosphere. Rocks which do hit the Earth are called meteorites.

Craters on the Moon were made by meteorites.

The largest meteorite crater on Earth, in Arizona, USA. It is over 1 km across.

Eclipses and Auroras

When the Moon passes between the Sun and the Earth, it blocks off most of the Sun's light. This is called a solar eclipse. When the Earth passes between the Sun and the Moon, it cuts off most of the Sun's light from the Moon. This is called a lunar eclipse.

(Left) A solar eclipse. (Right) A lunar eclipse.

An Aurora appears when electrical particles from the Sun become trapped in the Earth's atmosphere.

People living in or near the Arctic Circle can often see ghostly, twisting curtains of light, called the Aurora Borealis, in the night sky. Similar lights, the Aurora Australis, are seen near the Antarctic.

Sky watching

Wear warm clothes when you go out at night. You will need a light to look at the star charts in this book.
Take a comfortable chair.

Mercury Saturn
Venus
Mars
Jupiter
Jupiter's moons

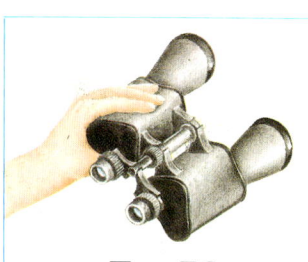

7 × 50 binoculars are fine for looking at the sky if you do not have a telescope.

These views are what you might see through a telescope. The planets seem to change size as they move nearer or further from Earth in their orbits.

To photograph the night sky, keep the camera still by supporting it on a tripod or against a wall. The camera must have a "B" setting. Use film with a rating of ISO 400. Expose for about 10 seconds. A picture like this one can be taken by pointing the camera at the Pole Star and leaving the shutter open for over an hour.

Safety note

You must **NEVER** look at the Sun through a telescope or binoculars. If you do so, you will be blinded.

The northern skies

Use the star map here and on page 29 to help you pick out the main constellations (groups of stars which form patterns or shapes) in the night sky. To use the star maps, turn the book until the present month is at the bottom. You should be able to see most of the stars in the middle and upper part of the star map.

The constellations

1 Andromeda
2 Aquarius
3 Aquila
4 Aries
5 Auriga
6 Bootes
7 Cancer
8 Canis Major
9 Canis Minor
10 Capricornus
11 Cassiopeia
12 Centaurus
13 Cepheus
14 Cetus
15 Columba
16 Corona Borealis
17 Corvus
18 Cygnus
19 Draco
20 Eridanus
21 Gemini

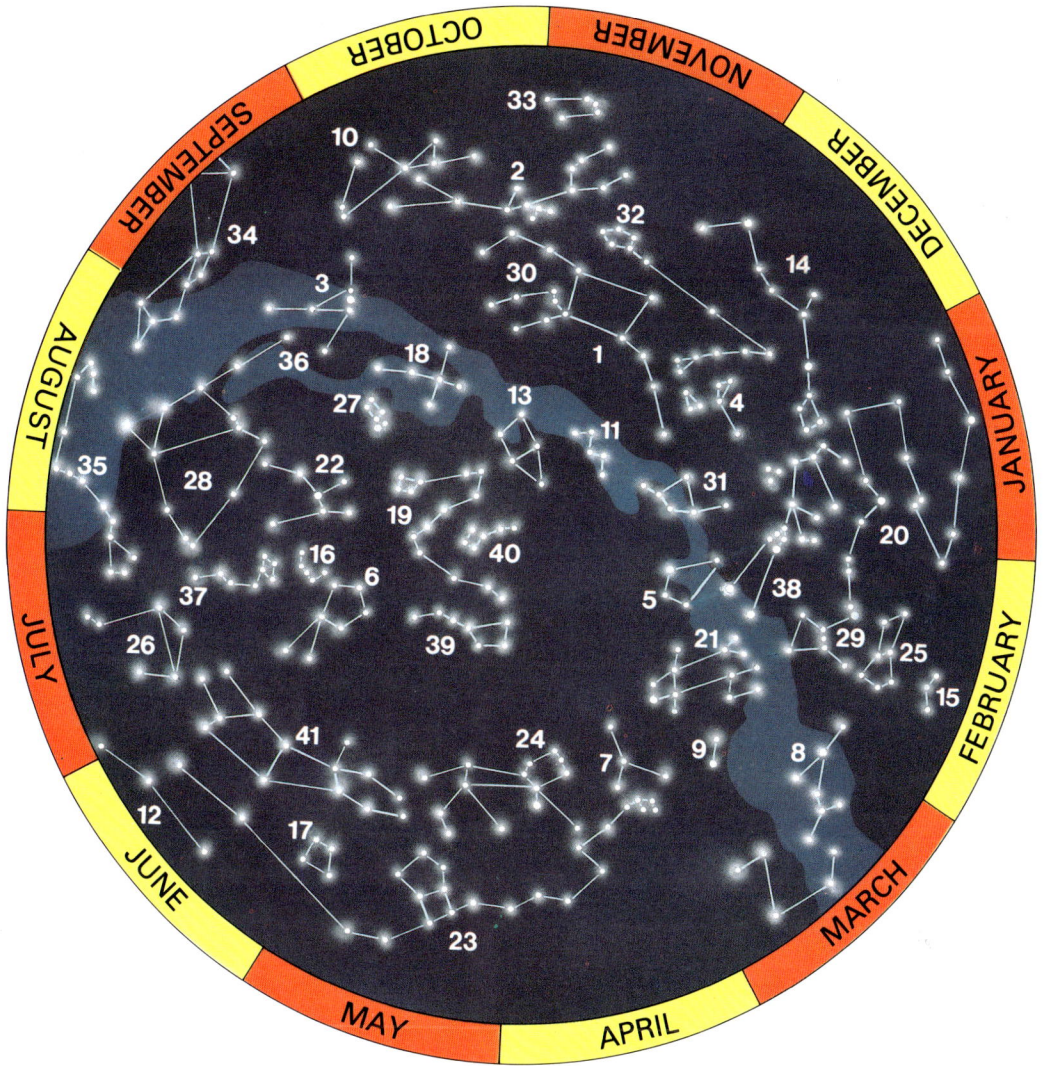

22 Hercules	29 Orion	36 Serpens Caput
23 Hydra	30 Pegasus	37 Serpens Cauda
24 Leo	31 Perseus	38 Taurus
25 Lepus	32 Pisces	39 Ursa Major
26 Libra	33 Pisces Austrinus	40 Ursa Minor
27 Lyra	34 Sagittarius	41 Virgo
28 Ophiucus	35 Scorpius	

The southern skies

This star map shows the constellations which can be seen in the southern half of the world. Crux, the Southern Cross, is the smallest but the easiest to spot. The brightest star in the southern skies is Sirius in Canis Major. You can find it by following the angle of the three stars in the middle of Orion, the Hunter.

The constellations

1 Ara
2 Aries
3 Aquarius
4 Aquila
5 Cancer
6 Canis Major
7 Canis Minor
8 Capricornus
9 Carina
10 Centaurus
11 Cetus
12 Corona Borealis
13 Corvus
14 Crater
15 Crux
16 Cygnus
17 Delphinus
18 Eridanus
19 Gemini
20 Grus
21 Hercules
22 Hydra
23 Leo
24 Libra

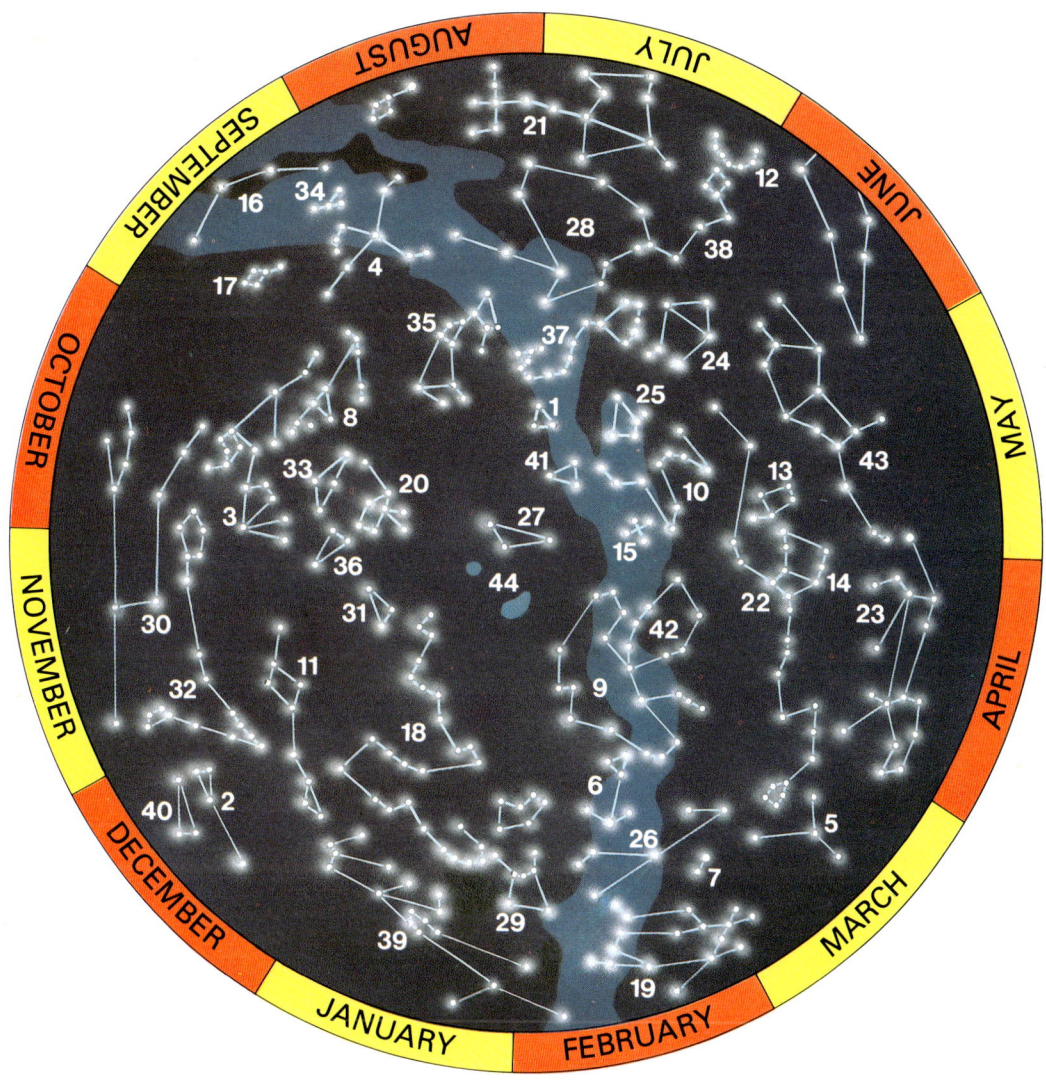

25 Lupus	32 Pisces	39 Taurus
26 Monoceros	33 Pisces Austrinus	40 Triangulum
27 Octans	34 Sagitta	41 Triangulum Australe
28 Ophiucus	35 Sagittarius	
29 Orion	36 Sculptor	42 Vela
30 Pegasus	37 Scorpius	43 Virgo
31 Phoenix	38 Serpens	44 Magellanic Clouds

*The pale blue band is the Milky Way.

Night sky facts

If it were possible to drive through space, it would take you 193 years to reach the Sun travelling at a speed of 88km per hour (55mph).

One of Jupiter's moons is the fastest moon in the Solar System. It travels round the planet in just over seven hours.

The light from the Sun takes eight minutes to reach the Earth.

The nearest star outside our Solar System is Proxima Centauri. It is over four light years away.

The temperature of the surface of the Sun is about 6,000°C. It is about 15 million °C in the centre.

About three or four meteors the size of your fist enter the Earth's atmosphere every day.

When you look up at the night sky, the stars seem to twinkle. In fact, stars shine with a steady light. They only appear to twinkle because their light is distorted as it passes through the Earth's atmosphere.

The only person known to have been hit by a meteorite is an American lady. In November 1954, a meteorite weighing 4kg (9lb) crashed through her roof, bounced off a radio and struck her on the hip. She was badly bruised, but suffered no permanent injury.

The largest known meteorite to hit the Earth landed in Arizona, USA, in prehistoric times. It was the size of a house.

Glossary

Here is the meaning of some of the words used in this book:

Atmosphere
The layer of gas round a planet.

Constellation
A group of stars which seem to form a pattern.

Crater
A large hole in the ground made by a meteorite.

Eclipse
When one body passes into the shadow of another. A lunar eclipse happens when the shadow of the Earth falls on the Moon, cutting off the sunlight.

Light year
The distance light travels in one year. It is about 9.5 million km or 5.9 million miles.

Orbit
The path in which a small object repeatedly travels round a larger one. The Moon orbits the Earth once a month. The Earth orbits the Sun once a year.

Planet
A heavenly body which travels in orbit round a sun.

Spaceprobe
An unmanned spacecraft which carries telescopes and cameras for observing planets and stars.

Star
A glowing ball of gas in space. The nearest star to Earth is the Sun.

Index

Atmosphere 13, 14, 16, 20, 30, 31
Aurora Australis 23
Aurora Borealis 23

Binoculars 24, 25

Comet 18, 19, 20
Constellations 7, 26, 27, 28, 29, 31
Crater 10, 12, 21, 31

Earth 8, 9, 10, 12, 13, 14, 20, 21, 22, 23, 24, 30, 31
Eclipse 22, 31

Galaxy 5, 6,
Giotto 19
Great Red Spot 14

Halley's Comet 19

Jupiter 9, 14, 24, 30

Light year 30, 31

Mars 9, 12, 13, 24
Mercury 9, 12, 24
Meteor 20, 30
Meteorite 20, 21, 30, 31

Milky Way 6, 29
Moon 10, 11, 16, 21, 22, 31
Moons 8, 9, 16, 17, 24, 30

Neptune 9, 16, 17

Orbit 10, 25, 31

Planets 8, 9, 12, 14, 15, 16, 24, 30, 31
Pluto 9, 16

Rings 14, 15, 16

Saturn 9, 14, 15, 24
Solar System 8, 9, 14, 30
Space 4, 10, 18, 30, 31
Spacecraft 13, 31
Spaceprobe 12, 17, 19, 31
Star 4, 5, 6, 7, 16, 24, 25, 26, 28, 30, 31
Sun 6, 8, 9, 10, 16, 18, 19, 22, 23, 25, 30, 31

Telescope 4, 12, 16, 24, 25, 31

Universe 5
Uranus 9, 16, 17

Venus 9, 12, 13, 24
Voyager 15, 17